FINDING a CAREER

Careers If You Like Government and Politics

Michael V. Uschan

ReferencePoint Press®

San Diego, CA

Dedication
This book is dedicated to Joyce Meyer, Rev. Jeffrey T. LaBelle, Lisa Meincke, Craig Gilbert, Lewis A. Lukens, and Joel Dietl for sharing their job experiences with me for this book.

About the Author
Michael V. Uschan has written nearly one hundred books, including *Life of an American Soldier in Iraq*, for which he won the 2005 Council for Wisconsin Writers Juvenile Nonfiction Award. It was the second time he won the award. Uschan began his career as a writer and editor with United Press International, a wire service that provided stories to newspapers, radio, and television. He and his wife, Barbara, reside in the Milwaukee suburb of Franklin, Wisconsin.

Picture Credits
Cover: Depositphotos
12: Thinkstock Images
36: Depositphotos
52: Thinkstock Images
69: Thinkstock Images

© 2017 ReferencePoint Press, Inc.
Printed in the United States

For more information, contact:
ReferencePoint Press, Inc.
PO Box 27779
San Diego, CA 92198
www.ReferencePointPress.com

LIBRARY OF CONGRESS CATALOGING-IN-PUBLICATION DATA

Name: Uschan, Michael V., 1948- author.
Title: Careers if you like government and politics / by Michael V. Uschan.
Description: San Diego, CA : ReferencePoint Press, Inc., 2017. | Series: Finding a career | Audience: Grade 9-12. | Includes bibliographical references and index.
Identifiers: LCCN 2016004071 (print) | LCCN 2016016151 (ebook) | ISBN 9781682820001 (hardback) | ISBN 9781682820018 (eBook)
Subjects: LCSH: Political science--Vocational guidance--United States--Juvenile literature. | Vocational guidance--United States--Juvenile literature.
Classification: LCC JA88.U6 U64 2017 (print) | LCC JA88.U6 (ebook) | DDC 324.023/73--dc23
LC record available at https://lccn.loc.gov/2016004071

CONTENTS

Introduction: Stuck on Government and Politics

Some people live by the adage "Never discuss politics or religion in polite company." Others thrive on political discourse. They're glued to Internet news feeds during election season and never miss a candidate debate. They run for student government and volunteer in the community every chance they get. They hang on every tweet from a politician or political organization—and sometimes reply with a few choice words of their own. Government is one of their favorite subjects in school and they can never get enough of local, national, or global politics. Does any of this sound familiar? If so, you might want to consider a career that builds on your fascination with and study of government and politics.

Elective office is one avenue, of course. Elected officials work in many capacities of local, state, and national government. By some estimates, there are at least half a million elected positions at all three levels of government. At the local level, elected officials serve on city councils, county commissions, and school boards. They also hold office as city auditors, county clerks, and treasurers. At the state level, elected officials make laws as members of legislatures and hold executive positions like governor, state treasurer, or superintendent of schools. And at the national level, elected officials include the president and members of Congress.

Critical Thinkers Have Many Options

But so many other career possibilities exist for people who like government and politics. The study of politics and political systems is called political science. Political science, according to the political science department website of the University of California, Davis, "concerns not only the institutions of government but also the analysis of such phenomena as political behavior, political values, political change and stability, parties, pressure groups, bureaucracies, administrative behavior, justice, national security, and international affairs."

Those who study any or all of these subjects develop certain skills and abilities. The number one skill is critical thinking. The ability to "gather information and opinions through a variety of means and synthesize the findings into a coherent and persuasive argument" is central to the study of political science, according to the website of the College of Arts and Sciences at the University of Kentucky. It's also a key element in critical thinking, along with problem solving and the ability to understand opposing views. Strong communication skills, both written and verbal, are among other characteristics that develop through the study of government and politics.

These skills and abilities are in demand in many careers, including those found in nonelective positions in local, state, and national government. Other possibilities include international aid organizations, political campaigns, interest groups and lobbying organizations, journalism, business, and law. The list of jobs that require critical thinking, problem solving, a knack for understanding different perspectives, and strong writing and speaking skills is long. A few areas that might not come immediately to mind are public administration, human relations, social work, public policy research, law enforcement, and even sales and marketing.

Working for the Public Good

People who study and enjoy learning about government and politics have different reasons for the career choices they make. One of the most common reasons is the desire to do work for the public good. That is why Joyce Meyer became a congressional staffer. Meyer served as deputy chief of staff for Representative Paul Ryan (R-WI) in 2015. In an interview with the author, Meyer said, "I always knew I wanted to work in public service." Meyer's parents had immigrated to the United States from the Philippines. She said public service was her way of repaying the United States for the opportunity it had given her parents to have a better life.

Those who study government and politics tend to also have a strong interest in learning about and understanding other cultures—and not just from books. In an interview with the author, Lewis A. Lukens said he became a Foreign Service officer for the US State Department because of "wanderlust, a desire to travel and see the world." His travels as a diplomat took him to many countries, including Iraq, Australia, and China. There is no better way to truly learn about another culture than to be immersed in it. This experience can also lead to a deeper understanding of one's own culture—and ultimately to an exchange of ideas and knowledge. This was another reason Lukens chose to work in the Foreign Service: He wanted to help people in other countries gain a better understanding of his own country.

A fascination with government and politics can also lead to a career that revolves around helping people negotiate the complexities of government rules and regulations. Lawyers often play this role for their clients, which means they have to be willing to dig into the intricacies of government. Becoming a lawyer might also allow you to deal with issues about which you care deeply. Legal disputes involve an endless number of subjects, and you can choose to practice law in an area that excites you. Florida attorney Renata Castro became an immigration lawyer because she knew how much immigrating to the United States from her native Brazil had changed her own life. Castro said in a 2015 newspaper story, "I love being able to participate in people's dreams to move to the USA lawfully."

If learning about the law or working in a foreign country is not your thing, don't fret. Your interest in government and politics can serve you equally well in another profession—teaching. Think about it: Teachers help develop young minds. They help lay the groundwork for young people who will one day become full participants in society. You can't get any more grass roots than that. Lisa Meincke is a third-grade teacher at Lakeview Elementary School in Whitewater, Wisconsin. In an interview with the author, she said, "I wanted to feel fulfilled in my career. So, after a lot of thought, I decided to pursue education knowing I wanted to educate children and make a difference in their lives."

Or maybe you're a person who likes to solve problems. Your studies of government and politics have taught you to look beyond the obvious, to understand and analyze various perspectives, and to assess the effects of action and reaction. And when you want to be, you can be very persuasive. These are some of the skills that are required of urban planners such as Joel Dietl. Dietl is the planning manager for the city of Franklin, Wisconsin. Dietl's job allows him to use his analytical skills to fix problems and his persuasive skills to build support for projects he wants to see done. An added plus of the job: he's never bored. In an interview with the author, Dietl said: "I didn't want a job that would be nine to five and was one that I couldn't wait until the clock hit five so I could go home. I wanted to do something I liked that would interest me for the rest of my life."

Journalism is a good profession for people interested in how politics and government work. That is because it is the job of a journalist to explain to the general public what is happening in those two areas. The reporting that journalists do is also vital to democracy because they serve as watchdogs to make sure government officials are doing their jobs legally and properly. Craig Gilbert is based in Washington, DC, and reports on national politics for the *Milwaukee Journal Sentinel* newspaper. In an interview with the author, Gilbert said he chose a career in journalism because he "was interested in politics and public affairs and I also liked to write." His job satisfies his interest in all three areas.

There are many jobs in which your interest in politics and government can make the work you do both enjoyable and meaningful. All you have to do—like the people mentioned above—is find one that excites you and fits your talents.

Congressional Staffer

Washington, DC, has the reputation of being one of the most thrilling places to work because what happens there can affect people living in all fifty states—and even the entire world. Representatives and senators have budgets to hire staff in offices they maintain in Washington, DC, and in offices they operate in the states and districts they represent. Many people interested in government and politics dream of becoming a congressional staffer because they believe that being at the center of national politics and government is exciting. They also think such work is meaningful because what they do when they help to create new programs, for example, has the potential to help people in their daily lives. Patriotism is another reason for becoming a congressional staffer; the idea of playing a part in the workings of government appeals to people who see government as crucial to how the nation functions.

The satisfaction congressional staffers have in their jobs is high; in fact, most love their work. A recent survey of more than fourteen hundred congressional staff workers revealed that 79 percent of respondents were excited about their jobs, 94 percent wanted to continue their work because they believed it was meaningful, and 90 percent believed their jobs were a valuable form of public service.

What Does a Congressional Staffer Do?

Congressional staffers generally work in one of two main groups: personal staff or committee staff. Personal staffers work either in Washington or in the congressperson's home state or district. These staffers handle the needs of constituents, help draft legislation, deal with the news media, coordinate the congressperson's schedule, and meet with individuals, lobbyists, and larger groups advocating positions on various issues. Each member of Congress is assigned to several committees that deal with legislation on topics such as education or health care. This is where committee staffers work. Committee staffers keep their bosses informed on bills the committee is considering and offer advice on the economic and political pluses and minuses of those bills.

Whether working as personal or committee staff, congressional staffers rely on certain key skills. They must be able to do research and understand complex topics. Critical thinking is essential, as is the ability to communicate effectively with different types of people.

There are a wide variety of staff jobs, each carrying different levels of responsibility. Staff assistant is an entry-level job that

What Motivates Congressional Staffers?

"Working for Congress is a way for me to serve my country. Congress needs smart and principled individuals who are willing to sacrifice some part of their lives [to] make our country work better, and I'm proud to be a part of that."

Quoted in Congressional Management Foundation and the Society for Human Resource Management, *Life in Congress: Job Satisfaction and Engagement of House and Senate Staff*, 2013. www.congressfoundation.org.

usually involves dealing with telephone and e-mail requests and clerical duties like typing and faxing documents. Field representatives, also known as caseworkers, handle more substantive tasks. They keep their bosses informed on how local, federal, and state officials are handling important issues. Sometimes they even make recommendations on what action to take on them. Other congressional staffer jobs include district director, a position that oversees activity at the congressperson's home office, and press secretary, the staffer who interacts with the news media. Chief of staff is the highest congressional staff job. This person oversees staff in a congressperson's Washington and home offices, manages the congressperson's strategy on legislative issues, and is one of the congressperson's top policy advisers.

Some of the staff duties may seem unimportant. However, Representative James McGovern (D-MA) believes that staffers are vital to a congressperson's success. In a 2013 *Washington Times* story, McGovern said, "Any member who tells you they do it on their own is not being honest. We're inundated with thousands of issues, and to be a productive member of Congress you need your staff." One reason McGovern appreciates his staffers is that he began his political career as one.

Even the simplest tasks that congressional staffers perform can have importance beyond their obvious outcomes. Arranging a White House tour for a constituent, for example, can elicit gratitude, which can turn into a vote for the congressperson in the next election. (And winning reelection is vitally important to members of Congress.)

How Do You Get a Congressional Staffer Job?

Most representatives employ up to fourteen full-time and four part-time staffers, but senators may hire as many as thirty-four staffers. Competition for staffer jobs is stiff because they are in high demand. A college degree is a necessity. A degree in political science is especially helpful because it shows that you are knowledgeable about politics and government. It is not a requirement,

Compiling Briefing Books

"I write memos on controversial bills—covering the pros, the cons, who supports the bill, and who's against it; and I make a recommendation on how to vote . . . I attend markup sessions with my boss, and if there are important issues, I put together briefing books that contain talking points or statements for [him] to make during the markups. If [the congressman's] going to offer an amendment, I draft it and compile supporting information."

Quoted in Steve Seidenberg, "The View from the Hill: Working as a Congressional Staffer," Law Crossing. www.lawcrossing.com.

however, and a degree in many other majors, including economics, can be useful in staff positions.

If you know that someday you'd like to get a position as a congressional staffer, you can improve your chances even while you're still in high school. Participation in student government and volunteering on election campaigns can provide a valuable introduction to the world of politics. Both the House of Representatives and the Senate also have unpaid intern positions for high school students. All of these activities look good on a résumé and may lead to personal contacts who might be able to help you one day get that staffer job.

A good way to start job hunting is by contacting members of Congress from your hometown or state because they are more likely to hire someone from the area they represent. But you can also check job listings posted by the Senate and the House of Representatives. *Roll Call* and the *Hill*, two influential newspapers available online that report on Congress, also list such jobs. The papers are good sources of information on how Congress works. Occasionally they even run articles that examine how various members of Congress treat their staffs.

Personal Qualities That Matter

Congressional staffers interact with many different types of people. They range from high-ranking elected and government officials—maybe even the president—to lobbyists and average people who are constituents. Staffers must be personable and friendly; they must be able to treat all visitors with respect and make them feel at ease. Every personal contact a staffer makes is vitally important because it reflects on the image of the member of Congress whom he or she represents. Staffers also must be able to follow orders, carry them out exactly, and remain enthusiastic even while doing minor tasks.

Congressional staffers should be adept at communicating through various types of social media. Staffers, however, have to be careful about their tweets and Internet postings. In 2014 Elizabeth Lauten, the communications director for Representative Stephen Fincher (R-TN), criticized the teenage daughters of President Barack Obama when they appeared at the annual

Congressional staffers see politics in action every day. During congressional hearings, they may take notes on remarks made by members of Congress who are considering changes on proposed bills.

White House Thanksgiving ceremony in which the president pardons a turkey. On Facebook, Lauten scolded Malia and Sasha for looking bored. Lauten wrote, "Rise to the occasion. Act like being in the White House matters to you. Dress like you deserve respect, not a spot at a bar." Republicans have often criticized Obama because he is a Democrat. However, political figures of both parties are in general agreement that family members—especially children—are off-limits for such criticism. Lauten had to resign a few days later because of the backlash over her ill-advised posting.

The Best and Worst Parts of the Job

Congressional staffers get a firsthand look at government and politics in action—and sometimes they become active participants in either or both depending on what their jobs entail. The feeling that you're doing something important—something that matters—is a good one. Carter Moore was a staffer for several years for both Representative Julia Carson (D-IN) and the House Committee on Veteran Affairs. Moore is now a senior policy adviser on health care in Australia. In a 2013 article for the online magazine *Slate*, Moore recalled the pride he felt about the work he did as a staffer: "I was and remain extraordinarily proud of the time I spent working in Congress."

Working as a congressional staffer can be rewarding, but the job is not easy and the hours are often longer than the usual forty-hour workweek. When Keenan Austin was a senior policy aide to Representative Frederica Wilson (D-FL), her days often lasted more than twelve hours. Lunch was usually just a sandwich she quickly gobbled down while going from one task to another. In a 2014 news story in the *Hill*, a House staffer complained that the long hours made it hard to have a life outside of work: "These days we just work, work, work . . . in terribly crowded and inadequate facilities with no privacy, for extremely long hours. [These] jobs are very hard on family life, and frankly, I'm getting tired of it." And although most staffers are off on weekends and major holidays,

Life with Low Pay

"[The] salary was not at all generous. [Most] staffers I know and worked with live with many housemates, many of whom were also congressional staff, in order to be able to live and work in Washington on an entry-level staffer's salary. [This] does add significantly to staffers' stress, as they're living in one of the most expensive cities in the U.S."

Quoted in Carter Moore, "What Is Daily Life Like for a Member of Congress or Congressional Staffer?," *Slate*, November 7, 2013. www.slate.com.

their schedule is largely dictated by Congress; when Congress is in session, staffers are sure to be at their jobs too.

Congressional staffers also need a thick skin. When they head home, or even sometimes on the job, they're likely to hear a variety of negative comments about Congress and the job it has done—or hasn't done. As a hardworking staffer, those comments can be frustrating and even hurtful, but everyone knows they are one of the hazards of the job.

One other job hazard has to do with longevity. Even if you are a very good worker, your job will be in jeopardy every time your boss is up for reelection. If he or she loses, so do you.

Most Congressional Staffers Aren't in It for the Money

Working as a congressional staffer can be exciting and emotionally rewarding, but the pay may be disappointing. Staff assistant, an entry-level job, is the most common staff position. The median pay for that job is $30,000—which is pretty low for a place like Washington, DC, which has a high cost of living. Workers in higher-ranking jobs earn much more money. A chief of staff, for example, will likely make more than $150,000 a year. But even high-earning staffers generally have incomes much lower (20 to

14

30 percent lower) than people with similar education and skills who work in private-sector jobs. Low pay means high turnover: congressional staffers are often forced to search for better-paying jobs—sometimes with other members of Congress.

Is There a Future for Congressional Staffer Jobs?

The number of congressional staff jobs will remain the same unless Congress decides to trim or add such positions. Regardless, working as a congressional staffer can be a stepping-stone to other jobs. The experience and contacts staffers make can be invaluable—both in other careers and for those who have a desire to someday run for political office. In January 2015 Representative Ryan became Speaker of the House, a powerful position in Congress. He began his political career in 1992 as a staffer for then-senator Robert Kasten Jr. (R-WI). Ryan is by no means the only member of Congress who started his political career that way. In 2015 he was just one of 102 members of Congress who had worked as congressional staffers early in their careers. Staffers who don't want to run for office often have plenty of options as well. They frequently land jobs in federal, state, or local government. Their experience also makes them highly valued for work in just about any field in the private sector.

Find Out More

American Political Science Association
website: www.apsanet.org

The American Political Science Association is the leading professional organization for the study of political science. Its website includes a section on career options for undergraduate and graduate students in political science. Potential earnings, internships, and other career information is included.

Congressional Institute
website: http://conginst.org

This nonprofit corporation has information that helps members of Congress. It also has blogs on how Congress operates and information on available jobs and how to find housing when you get a job.

USAJOBS
website: www.usajobs.gov

The federal government's official source for job listings is a free web-based job board enabling federal job seekers access to thousands of job opportunities across hundreds of federal agencies and organizations, including Congress.

US House of Representatives Human Resources Office
263 Cannon House Office Building
Independence and S. Capitol Sts. SE
Washington, DC 20515
phone: (202) 225-2450
website: www.house.gov

This website has information on members of Congress, how Congress operates, and internships available to students interested in working for Congress.

US Senate Placement Office
142 Hart Senate Office Building
Second and Constitution Aves. NE
Washington, DC 20510
phone: (202) 224-9167
website: http://www.senate.gov/visiting/common/generic/placement_office.htm

This part of the US Senate website has information on jobs with senators. The jobs include internships for high school juniors who are at least sixteen years old.

Foreign Service

Working in a foreign country requires a certain kind of person—someone who is patient, resourceful, adaptable, and good at solving problems. Working for the US Foreign Service requires those same qualities—and more. Foreign Service officers need to be knowledgeable about US and global politics, history, and geography; have a basic understanding of economics and the legal system; and demonstrate solid communication and interpersonal skills. Notice anything? These are the very same qualities and skills you develop and nurture as you pursue your passion for politics and government.

Working in a Foreign Country

Foreign Service officers working around the world perform a valuable service for their country. Living and working thousands of miles away from the United States, they directly manage and implement the nation's diplomatic relationships. Those relationships are vital to the economic and political well-being of the United States as well as its security from military or terrorist attacks. The State Department website sums up the job this way: "The mission of a Foreign Service [officer] is to promote peace, support prosperity, and protect American citizens while advancing the interests of the U.S. abroad."

The Foreign Service employs thirteen thousand people in more than 270 diplomatic missions around the world; that number includes both Foreign Service officers and Foreign Service specialists. The job of Foreign Service officer can vary widely, depending on need and location. Sometimes Foreign Service officers meet with officials and citizens of other countries to discuss common interests or to ease problems between nations. Sometimes they are involved in efforts to organize free elections, improve educational and health care systems, reform judicial systems, and help people recover from natural disasters. Not all of the work of Foreign Service officers is quite so heady. Sometimes their job is simply to help US citizens who have encountered problems while living or traveling in foreign countries. Serious illness, a lost passport, or legal problems of various sorts can be daunting to deal with when you don't speak the language or understand how things work. These are some of the things Foreign Service officers help with when the need arises.

Julie Ruterbories enjoyed Foreign Service work because she was able to aid fellow Americans encountering problems in foreign

Much More than a Job

"The U.S. Foreign Service is really more than just a job, it is a lifestyle. You can see the world and will have some of the best stories to share. I had the opportunity to listen to Magic Johnson tell stories about his rivalry with Larry Bird. I scoured the markets of [Kiev], Ukraine once for caffeine-free Diet Pepsi for a Secretary of State. I listened to a Haitian man seeking a U.S. visa explain to me that his fingerprints had fallen off during the earthquake and that must be why my computer said he had a criminal record."

Shawn Kobb, "So You Want My Job: Foreign Service Officer/Diplomat," April 25, 2013. www.artofmanliness.com.

countries. In a 2014 interview with the *Chronicle*, Duke University's student newspaper, Ruterbories said, "I'm able to look back and know that I've made a difference. That I've touched somebody's life and know that I made a difference." An example of such service was when an American died in a plane crash in Kyrgyzstan. Ruterbories, who was stationed there, notified the widow and arranged for the man's body to be transported home.

So You Want to Be a Foreign Service Officer?

The life of a Foreign Service officer can be exotic and adventurous. Lewis A. Lukens served in many countries as a Foreign Service officer, including Iraq, Senegal, and Canada. He even traveled more than 50,000 miles (80,467 km) with Secretary of State Hillary Clinton when she visited various nations. In an interview with the author, Lukens said he loved his work because he felt he was "doing important work while having the incredible opportunity to travel and live in countries around the world." Immersion in other countries and cultures allows Foreign Service officers to see politics and government at work in many different settings. Plus, this job offers opportunities you just don't get in other run-of-the-mill jobs—like taking an elephant ride.

Foreign Service officers work in five separate career tracks. Consular officers help US citizens living or traveling overseas deal with issues like adopting foreign children. Economic officers work with foreign officials on technology, trade, the environment, and other key issues. Management officers direct operations of the nation's embassies around the world, performing such tasks as buying property and managing personnel. Political officers analyze political activity in the country in which they're stationed. Public diplomacy officers meet and work with foreign government officials and public and private citizens and groups to influence public opinion and promote understanding and support for US policy goals.

The increased threat of terrorist attacks overseas and at home in recent years has created a new and important task for Foreign Service officers—keeping the United States safe. Some officers are involved in the tracking of terrorists and other efforts aimed at preventing them from causing harm.

The Foreign Service also hires people to work as Foreign Service specialists. A specialist has skills in areas such as administration, office management, information technology, and construction— and they work closely with Foreign Service officers.

How Do You Get into the Foreign Service?

There is no particular college major to pursue for joining the Foreign Service. The State Department has a Diplomats in Residence (DIR) program that recruits Foreign Service workers. In 2015 former Foreign Service officers were stationed in fifteen colleges throughout the nation as part of the program's outreach efforts. Contacting the DIR representative nearest you would be a good way to learn about a job in the Foreign Service. Linda Cheatham once headed the DIR program. In a 2012 interview with the *U.S. News & World Report*, she said students with almost any major can apply: "One of my colleagues [said], 'Make sure that your diplomats in residence tell people that we don't need everyone to be an international affairs major.'" Most Foreign Service workers must have the ability to master the language of the countries to which they are assigned. Taking a foreign language course will prove you have that ability.

Foreign Service candidates must be between the ages of twenty and fifty-nine. The first step in applying for this job is to take the Foreign Service Officer Test, which measures a candidate's knowledge, skills, and abilities. The test is both multiple choice and essay and covers a variety of subjects, including US culture, US government, US and world history, economics, and technology. The essay portion tests a candidate's ability to write concisely, a key skill for the job. The test is very difficult. However, applicants can take it several times until they pass it. The hiring process includes writing a personal life narrative, an oral quiz, and medical and security clearance checks. A review panel then considers each applicant to see if he or she is suitable for the job.

One Hardship of Foreign Service

"The most exciting thing about my job is also the most challenging. Moving from country to country, starting a new job, meeting new people, and trying to get to know the country/ culture. It's super fun [but] very hard to leave your family behind. [I] would say the most difficult thing was saying goodbye for the first time."

Ana Escrogima, quoted in Libby Rothberg, "Careers in the Foreign Service—One Diplomat's Story," July 20, 2015. www.collegerecruiter.com.

Personal Qualities That Matter Most

If you plan to pursue a Foreign Service career, the first rule is that you have to like traveling—because Foreign Service officers are moved to new assignments about every three years. And you have to be adaptable—because with that much moving around you're likely to be switching cities or countries right about the time you start to get comfortable. An interest in other cultures and a willingness to learn about other ways of life are also high on the must-have qualities list. Fluency in other languages—or at least the ability to master them at a conversational level—counts for a lot too. So does the ability to think and communicate clearly and calmly regardless of whatever chaos may be going on around you. In an interview with the author, Foreign Service officer Lukens said being able to handle unexpected problems or situations is very important: "This is a job where unexpected things happen a lot and you have to be able to roll with the punches."

The Good and Bad Parts of the Job

The opportunity to travel the world and learn firsthand about different cultures is probably the best part of the job. Foreign Service officer Ruterbories admits that moving every few years to a new country to work can be hard because she has to leave behind friends, learn new languages, and adapt to new cultures. But it can also be thrilling. In a 2014 interview, Ruterbories said, "Adjusting to new environments can be challenging, but for me that has always been exciting." And on those occasions where people in this line of work feel they are influencing events (in a good way), that too can be very satisfying, as Foreign Service officer Ana Escrogima explained in a 2015 interview: "It's all about doing what I'm passionate about [and] making a difference in lives and local or global issues."

Although the job of a Foreign Service officer can be exciting and fulfilling, it isn't always. In an article for the online *Huffington Post* online newspaper, former Foreign Service officer Peter Van Buren describes some of the least satisfying work he was asked to do. It involved taking the wives of visiting US officials shopping or sightseeing.

What's more, life in some countries can be quite challenging—and sometimes downright scary. Foreign Service officers can be stationed in countries or regions that have inadequate supplies of healthy food and clean water, poor air quality, primitive sanitation systems, and inadequate housing. These conditions can make daily life exceedingly uncomfortable. And then there are the countries that are just plain dangerous. When Foreign Service officer Shawn Kobb was stationed in Kabul, Afghanistan, he had two sets of body armor to wear whenever he went into a conflict zone. Kobb also took classes in what to do if he was taken hostage by militants fighting to control that country. Likewise, when Lukens served in Baghdad, Iraq, from 2002 to 2005 he was in constant danger from rockets and mortars fired at the compound in which he lived. Sometimes, sadly, the bombers find their mark. In 2013, for instance, Foreign Service officer Anne Smedinghoff was killed by a suicide bomber in Afghanistan while she was delivering books to a school.

Earnings

In 2015 the entry-level salary for someone with a bachelor's degree started at $44,082, a master's at $49,311, and a doctorate at $60,855. Pay rises with promotions. Danger or hardship pay can also increase salary. This is given to people who are stationed in countries experiencing civil strife, terrorism, or war—such as Afghanistan and Iraq.

In addition to salary, the State Department pays travel expenses to assigned countries for Foreign Service officers and authorized family members and ships their personal belongings there. In foreign countries, officers live for free in government-leased housing or receive a housing allowance if there is no government housing. The government pays tuition for children to attend international schools, but officers must pay all other living expenses. Other benefits include life insurance, health care, a retirement savings plan, and ten paid holidays plus leave, which is capped at thirty days per year.

Future Job Opportunities

There are thirteen thousand Foreign Service officers working in more than 270 diplomatic missions around the world. Job opportunities will remain strong in the future. In 2015 the United States reopened diplomatic relations with Cuba, which created more Foreign Service positions, and foreign relations with all countries remains vital.

Find Out More

American Foreign Service Association (AFSA)
website: www.afsa.org

The AFSA, established in 1924, is the professional association and labor union of the US Foreign Service. This site explains how to get such jobs and explains what life is like for a Foreign Service officer.

Foreign Service Test
website: www.foreignservicetest.com

This site by former Foreign Service officer Shawn Kobb explains what the Foreign Service is like from the perspective of someone who knows.

State Magazine
website: www.state.gov/m/dghr/statemag

This is the website of the US State Department's magazine, which has articles about the Foreign Service.

US Department of State Careers
website: http://careers.state.gov

This site explains the job of a Foreign Service officer and includes a brochure that explains how to apply for the position.

International Development

In 2015 Paloma Adams-Allen was deputy assistant administrator for the Bureau for Latin America and the Caribbean of the US Agency for International Development (USAID). In a USAID blog, she writes, "I grew up in a tiny village in Jamaica, and I've known my whole life I wanted to help people." One way she has done that is to oversee hundreds of millions of dollars in loans to individuals in other countries so they could start small businesses. Those loans created jobs and strengthened the economies of countries like Colombia, Chile, and Brazil. Adams-Allen loves her job because she helps people escape poverty: "To be able to give little Palomas in the Americas a new lease on life— that's just phenomenal."

A Wide-Open Field

International development is a broad field that includes both government and nongovernment jobs. People who work in international development are involved in programs to eliminate poverty and improve economic opportunity in poor countries in Latin America, Africa, and Asia. They develop and run programs aimed at alleviating shortages of food, safe drinking water, educational opportunities, and medical care. They engage with others who are trying to address issues related to climate change, gender equality, and sexual violence. They even help nations learn how to more equitably and democratically govern their citizens.

Those who work in international development must be resourceful, practical, and adaptable. They must be politically and culturally aware. They must be able to identify problems and solve them. They must be able to understand different points of view and express their own ideas clearly and succinctly. And being able to communicate in the language of the country where they work is a big plus. All in all, international development can be a great fit for those who like and study government and politics and devote themselves to really learning about the world.

International development is sometimes confused with humanitarian aid, but they're not the same thing. Humanitarian aid organizations like the Red Cross, for example, generally respond to emergencies like floods, tornadoes, and earthquakes. They bring food and water and set up temporary shelters. International development, on the other hand, "carries a connotation of lasting change," one global development expert writes on the Center for Global Development blog. As an international development worker, instead of feeding hungry people, you might teach them

Travel to Exotic Places

"Experiencing other cultures is an attraction for most people who decide to work abroad [in international development]. Living in a new culture provides different perspectives and helps increase the understanding of others. And some see in international work a chance to share with others who do not have the high standard of living enjoyed in the United States."

Jill N. Lacey, "Working Abroad: Finding International Internships and Entry-Level Jobs," Bureau of Labor Statistics, Fall 2006. www.bls.gov.

better ways to farm so they won't ever go hungry again. Or you might establish schools in foreign countries to train doctors to meet the medical needs of their people rather than bringing in emergency medical supplies.

What Would You Do in International Development?

If you want a career in international development, you can work for government agencies, private businesses, or nonprofit organizations. Nonprofits include religious groups, charities, and other organizations that try to improve the common good of society by working for social change or to help specific groups of people. They are called nonprofits because any profit they make goes back into the work they do. You will find many international development jobs in the nonprofit sector. The United Nations (UN) is a nonprofit, and it performs more development work around the world than any other organization. Other nonprofits that work in international development include Doctors Without Borders, International Fund for Wildlife, Haiti Replacement Homes, and Child Empowerment International.

There are so many nonprofits doing development work that you can easily find one to work for that serves a cause that stirs your interest, ranging from fighting hunger to protecting women and children from sexual exploitation. And the possibilities of what kind of development work you will do are almost unlimited. Your job could be to meet with government officials in foreign countries to get their backing for development programs. Or you might teach local people how to purify contaminated water for their own use or oversee construction of plants that provide drinkable water for entire communities. In 2011, for example, international development worker Joan Hanawi helped people in Ecuador develop ways to trap rainwater so they would have safe, clean water for drinking, cooking, and other uses.

People with many types of educational backgrounds and skills work in international development. That is because many development projects are massive, requiring the expenditure of millions of dollars and years of work by many people. Those large projects require the services of many types of professionals, including engineers, accountants, lawyers, translators, public relations specialists, carpenters, and surveyors, among others.

How Do You Get into International Development?

If this sounds like your kind of career, you can begin preparing while you're still in high school. Studying one or more foreign languages is a good start, as is developing strong speaking and writing skills. Alanna Shaikh, who has worked in international development in many countries, says office skills are also useful. In a blog titled *Blood and Milk*, Shaikh recommended working in an office to prepare for development jobs because such work involves clerical tasks like filing reports. Working in an office can also teach you how to handle financial data and work with a team. In college, a major in international development will mean taking courses on global finance, economic development, and world cultures. Advanced degrees in this major will make it easier for you to find your first job. However, you can also major in computer technology, business, or education because international development programs also need people with such skills to accomplish their missions.

One way to get into the field when you graduate is to do volunteer work for an international development agency. Experience gained as a volunteer can be invaluable, both for gaining knowledge and for making contacts. Shaikh writes, "The paid opportunities will come in droves, but only after you distinguish yourself from the mass of inexperienced undergraduates who want to work abroad."

Dealing with the Quirks of the Job

As an international development worker, you should be willing to travel and meet different types of people. You also need to be able to adapt to living conditions—including climates and cuisines—that may be radically different from those to which you are accustomed. You need to be patient and resilient because many projects take a long time to show positive results, and some never succeed. Veteran development worker Hanawi said in a 2015 newspaper story, "For every success story, there is double the amount of failed projects." You need to be comfortable dealing with all kinds of people, from your fellow workers to foreign officials and the people you are trying to help. You should be confident enough in your abilities to remain calm and handle emergencies or unexpected problems that can occur no matter how well you plan a project.

The Good and Bad Parts of the Job

Perhaps the biggest reward of performing development work is the feeling of pride and satisfaction you will get from helping people. Traveling to exotic parts of the world, meeting new people, and experiencing things you never could have at home can be exciting. The bond you share with coworkers who have the same goal as you do can make even a difficult day at work easier to bear. In development work you may more quickly find yourself in a position of greater authority or responsibility at an early age, such as heading up a large project, than you would at many other jobs.

Living in a foreign country can be difficult because development work is done in poorer parts of the world. Basic living conditions

Fulfilling a Need

"This may sound obvious, but it is important to have skills, knowledge, or abilities that aid agencies need. . . . Engineers, agronomists, environmentalists, logisticians, linguists, and medical professionals are always in high demand because of their highly technical knowledge. . . . That said, social science majors and liberal arts students need not be discouraged. I was a history and religion major, which on the surface seems rather unhelpful. However, the skills that got my foot in the door were writing and research."

Matthew Bolton, "Becoming an Aid Worker," Transitions Abroad. www.transitionsabroad.com.

in some remote areas may be primitive, ranging from sleeping in tents to going without electricity. International development workers often have little or no access to adequate medical care, favorite foods, or the Internet. It can also be emotionally draining to be far away for long periods from family members and friends. In the worst possible scenario, a worker may be assigned to an area that is dangerous because of political or religious violence. In November 2015 Anita Datar of Takoma Park, Maryland, was one of twenty-seven people killed in a hotel in Mali by Islamist militants. She was a health specialist working for an international development company. The work can also be emotionally draining. In poor, undeveloped areas of the world, it can be difficult to be constantly exposed to the hardships that so many people endure. An international development worker's job is sometimes frustrating because workers do not have enough money or other resources to help all the hungry, sick, and abused people they encounter.

Earning a Living

Pay for international development workers varies depending on the employer and the type of work being done. Workers for USAID or other parts of government will receive salaries and benefits comparable to other government workers. And some of those salaries are quite respectable. At USAID in 2015 a program analyst earned $81,378 annually; a public health adviser, $97,890; and even interns earned $15.59 per hour. Salaries and benefits with charities and other organizations doing development work will vary according to their size and the amount of financing they have to perform their work.

Generally, however, development work pays less than many other jobs. No one goes into international development to get rich. Nick Macdonald is a veteran development worker. In his book *Getting Your First Job in Relief and Development*, he writes, "While there is a huge range of salaries and benefits [the] pay even at the top end with the United Nations and some contractors is generally less than the equivalent in the corporate world." However, some development employers offset lower wages with good benefits like health insurance and income supplements for housing or to educate children in a foreign country. Some development jobs also include help repaying or debt forgiveness for student loans.

A Vital, Ongoing Need

Ongoing political and religious conflicts and the extreme poverty that exists in many parts of the world are a guarantee that international development workers will continue to be vitally needed in the future. Government agencies, charities, and public and private organizations will all continue hiring to fulfill their missions of helping people in need.

Find Out More

Blood and Milk
website: http://bloodandmilk.org

This blog by Alanna Shaikh has information on international development work and careers.

Center for Global Development

website: www.cgdev.org

This organization conducts research and analysis on topics related to international development.

Center for International Development at Harvard University

website: www.hks.harvard.edu.centers.cid

This site has information on international development efforts around the world as well as education and careers in this field.

Devex

website: www.devex.com

This website, which features media reports, jobs, and links to other sites, tries to connect the global international development community.

Go Government

website: www.gogovernment.org

This website features information and tips on securing federal jobs, including those in international development.

UN Human Development Report 2015

website: http://hdr.undp.org/en/2015-report

This is the website for the UN's global report on international development programs and progress.

US Agency for International Development (USAID)

website: www.usaid.gov

This site describes the work of USAID, the agency that performs international development around the world.

Journalist

Journalism is a profession that revolves around information. Every day journalists provide their readers, listeners, and viewers with information about local, state, national, and world events. Journalists play an essential role in the American democratic system—and in all free societies. Whether working for online, print, or broadcast media, their job is to gather and report information on political, economic, and social events, ideas, and trends. They report on happenings, both large and small, that affect people's daily lives. They are the watchdogs of government and the voice of the people—even if "the people" don't always appreciate or agree with what's being reported.

Nevertheless, journalism is a natural fit for people who like government and politics. Craig Gilbert reports on government and politics from Washington, DC, for the *Milwaukee Journal Sentinel* newspaper. In an interview with the author, Gilbert said he loves his job. He believes the work he does is important—and meaningful: "It's my passion. There is a sense that what you're writing about is consequential. You have a sense of being part of history if you cover a major story. Part of the thrill of being a journalist is having that firsthand view when it comes to those kind of events."

Journalism is so important to democracy that the First Amendment to the US Constitution guarantees press freedom. It says, in part, that "Congress shall make no law . . . abridging the freedom of speech, or of the press." When the First Amendment was adopted on December 15, 1791, newspapers were the only form of news media. Since then, new technologies, including cameras, radio, television, computers, cell phones, and the Internet have allowed the delivery of news in ways the Founding Fathers could never have dreamed possible. But even journalists working with those new mediums are guaranteed the constitutional right to freely report news and express their opinions.

How Journalists Work

Thomas Kent is the deputy managing editor for the global news agency Associated Press. In a 2013 article on the *Huffington Post* website, Kent acknowledged that technology has changed how news is gathered and distributed. But, he says, the work journalists do remains the same: "Nothing has changed the journalist's fundamental job of reporting facts from the ground up— conducting original reporting, day after day, in a disciplined and consistent way." As a journalist reporting a story, you may see an event unfold in person or interview people who witnessed it. You may talk to people who can clarify what happened, why it happened, and what it means for the future. And then you'll do what journalists have always done—compile the information you gather in a format that enables your readers, viewers, or listeners to understand what's taking place and why.

News stories you write and pictures you take as a journalist today will be uploaded to the Internet as well as printed in newspapers and magazines. Or you may produce video and audio reports for television, radio, and the Internet. But whatever form your stories take and whatever technology disseminates them, the number one rule of journalism still applies—they must be accurate.

Journalists who work in all of the different media spend a lot of time chasing down leads for stories. Sometimes the stories work out; sometimes they don't. Depending on the type of story, a journalist may interview many people and review a lot of records before they can finish the story. Sometimes people they interview don't want to talk—although, surprisingly, many do want to share their thoughts even in the midst of tragedy. And sometimes the search for documents or witnesses that support a story can be difficult or impossible to obtain. Writing the story can also be challenging. Good stories almost never come easily, which is why perseverance is essential for any journalist.

Preparing for a Job in Journalism

Most journalists get degrees in journalism to prepare for this career. However, you don't need a journalism degree to become a reporter. Gilbert graduated from Yale University with a history degree. But his interest in government and politics and his writing ability led him into newspaper work, where he wound up covering government and politics in Washington, DC. Although a journalism degree can help you get a job as a journalist, a broad education is just as important because you may have to write stories about many different subjects. So a well-rounded education is a plus.

A good way to prepare for a journalism career and see if you would like it is to work on student newspapers (either print or online). Your school may even have a radio or television station to give you some experience. In recent decades, many newspapers have cut back on staff because of declining readership. As you get better at writing, you should contact local papers and other news media to see if they need help covering stories like a sporting event at your school. Even if you don't get paid for your work, it can be the beginning of your career as a journalist.

Personal Qualities and Essential Skills

Journalists must have certain qualities and skills. Magda Abu-Fadil has worked for decades for news organizations like Agence France-Presse and United Press International and has taught journalism at American University. In a 2015 blog on the site Media Helping Media, she discussed the qualities people need to succeed in journalism: "Curiosity, critical thinking, a hunger for

A journalist reports on participants in a marathon. Journalists get a firsthand view of events, both large and small, and have the opportunity to investigate and report on issues that have a direct effect on people's lives.

news, a burning desire to tell a good story, regardless of the medium or platform, and a dedication to accuracy, fairness, balance, and media ethics would be a good start."

The ability to organize facts and deliver an accurate story is the most important skill for a journalist. No matter what type of media they work for—print, broadcast, or online—journalists must be good communicators. They must be able to concisely, logically, and at times creatively explain the facts of stories they are communicating to their audience, whether that is through written or spoken words. They also need to be able to get information from many different types of people. That means not only knowing the right questions to ask but also how to ask them. At times it can be difficult to question someone who is emotional after a dramatic experience, such as a flood victim or an athlete after a big game. Journalists have to be sympathetic if people are frightened, angry, or even near tears with grief; otherwise, they may not share their information. For example, it is much easier to interview winners of sporting events than losers who may be upset and angry. Journalists also need to be savvy about communicating via social media such as Twitter so they can comment on news events while they are happening.

Journalists need to be able to handle the pressure of collecting facts and delivering their stories as fast as possible no matter what medium they're working in. In the past, journalists often had hours or even days to meet a story deadline depending on when their newspaper or magazine would be printed. But in the Internet age, stories are delivered almost instantaneously—often while events are still unfolding. That makes accuracy more challenging—and essential—than ever.

The Best and Worst Parts of the Job

Working as a journalist can be rewarding on many levels. For example, it feels good to know that people are reading, watching, or listening to the stories you developed. Watching events unfold before your eyes, and conveying the essence of those

Interviewing a President

"It can be a big adventure and very exciting. I got to interview President George W. Bush several times. Once was with several other reporters in the White House. And in 2005 I was invited to accompany him on *Air Force One* when he flew to Milwaukee. It was a one-on-one interview in his office [on the plane]. That was kind of cool, a place not too many people have been."

Craig Gilbert, quoted in an interview with the author, December 7, 2015.

events to others, can be exciting—whether it's a sporting event, a court trial, or a natural disaster. There is also a certain thrill that comes with interviewing well-known personalities or people who are at the forefront of a new medical discovery or political movement. And journalists who report on issues of importance to average people—for example, issues with affordable housing or education—get a great deal of satisfaction from their work.

And journalism isn't always thrilling. Your fascination with government and politics might not extend to fashion shows, groundbreakings for new construction, store openings, burglaries, car accidents, or the county fair. These and other events of daily life still have to be covered by journalists—usually by the youngest and newest on the job. Gere Goble is an editor for the *Mansfield (Ohio) News Journal*. In a 2015 column she listed some other drawbacks of being a journalist: "[They] work odd hours, holidays, weekends. When a story breaks, they're expected to drop everything and get to work. They don't expect to get rich off of it, either."

Other negative aspects include people who dislike your work criticizing you in letters, online comments, or e-mails. Electronic delivery of news has made it more important than ever to produce stories and deliver them to the public as fast as possible. The pressure you experience while trying to meet a deadline or get the story done as quickly as possible can also be nerve-racking. Some people you interview may be hard to deal with or even hostile because they dislike the news media or don't want to discuss what happened, such as an athlete whose mistake cost his or her team a victory or a politician caught lying. Those are just some of the things that can make getting your story done difficult.

However, the pressure of meeting a deadline can also be exhilarating. In a column that appeared in *Forbes* magazine, writer Jeff Bercovici, wrote: "Tracking down a scoop on deadline, when the newsroom is buzzing with dozens of people doing the same—it's an adrenaline rush. Plenty of jobs in this world offer the prospect of unrelieved boredom. I'd rather have one that gets my heart pumping."

How Much Can I Earn as a Journalist?

Although some journalists make a lot of money, journalism overall isn't one of the highest-paid professions. The amount you earn will depend on your job, experience, and the size of the company you work for. Median pay is the wage in which half the workers in a job earn less and half earn more than that salary. The US Bureau of Labor Statistics (BLS) reported that in 2014 the median pay for reporters and correspondents in newspapers was $40,810, and it was $49,640 in radio and television. However, median pay for broadcast news analysts—journalists who host news shows, read news, and comment on the news—was substantially higher at $85,120.

What Is the Future for Journalists?

Jobs in the print and broadcast media are declining because more people are now getting news from the Internet and social media. The BLS projects a 9 percent decline in print and broadcast reporting jobs by 2024. But don't lose heart if journalism is your passion. Many new online news formats, such as BuzzFeed and Vice, are being developed. Although this trend is expected to continue in the future, no one knows how big digital news will get. But because of that, you could be part of this new evolution in

Competition Is Fierce

"This is a competitive field. Period. It's competitive to get a job, especially now that there are fewer [journalism jobs]. It's competitive to keep the job you have and much more so to move up. It's performance based. On TV, you need ratings and major 'gets.' In print, you need big ideas, good relationships and solid writing. Online, you need traffic, social media audience, and compelling work."

Jenna Goudreau, "Top 10 Tips for Young Aspiring Journalists," *Forbes*, November 22, 2012. www.forbes.com.

journalism. And remember, there will always be a need for journalists to report the news because people have an insatiable curiosity about what is happening in the world.

Find Out More

American Press Institute
website: www.americanpressinstitute.org

The American Press Institute, based in Reston, Virginia, is an excellent source of information on all types of journalism.

Journalist's Toolbox
website: www.journaliststoolbox.org

This Society of Professional Journalism site has informative articles about journalism and links to other sites that can help aspiring journalists learn about this career.

School Journalism

website: www.schooljournalism.org

This site by the American Society of Newspaper Editors is a valuable resource for high school and college students working on school newspapers.

Society of Professional Journalists

website: www.spj.org

This site has information on journalism, jobs for journalists, and even videos to train journalists.

Lawyer

When people hear the word *lawyer,* what are the most likely images that come to mind? Probably they think of all of those lawyers they've seen on television. You know, the ones who are either superheroes or super diabolical? They're either hard-charging or soft-spoken, slimy or brilliant, ruthless or champions of the poor and disenfranchised, cunning or loaded with integrity. But that's television.

In the real world, lawyers are people who have an understanding of human nature. They're eloquent and able to think logically. They have the ability to sort through and critically analyze complicated information and circumstances. People who like and study government and politics possess and develop many of these same qualities, which is why so many of them gravitate to the legal profession. Many lawyers get into this profession because they want to help people who are facing legal difficulties. Justinian Lane is a personal injury lawyer in Seattle. In a blog on the Internet site Quora.com, Lane says, "I became a lawyer primarily because I wanted to help people. And that's the core part of why I like being a lawyer."

But no matter what type of law you choose or what kind of cases you take, the way you work will basically remain the same even though the details will change. Tyler G. Doyle is a partner in a Houston law firm that handles many types of cases. In a 2014 blog for Quora.com, Doyle wrote that he handles all of his cases in the same way: "You have to work hard, be dedicated to your craft, and committed to your clients. Good lawyers give maximum effort and attention to their clients, are constantly learning, and are always trying to get better at their work."

Criminal and Civil Law

If you want to become a lawyer, you'll have a wide variety of choices in the type of law to practice. You could become a government lawyer; agencies at all levels of government employ lawyers. Or you could work for a private firm. However, the main difference between lawyers—no matter whom they work for—is whether they specialize in criminal or civil law.

Criminal law involves actions—or crimes—that are considered harmful to society as a whole. This could include murder, kidnapping, robbery, sexual assault, driving under the influence, and fraud. Criminal lawyers are divided into two distinct groups—those who prosecute people for crimes and those who defend

We're Your Lawyer—Not Your BFF

"Sometimes, clients don't understand the role we must play as a lawyer, which often involves telling the client he or she is totally wrong or what the client wants isn't possible. Clients who don't get the answer they want will often think the attorney is acting against the client's interest. Also, clients sometimes have wildly unrealistic expectations from their lawyers."

Jeena Cho, "11 Reasons Why It's So Hard Being a Lawyer (Part 1)," Above the Law, June 11, 2015. http://abovethelaw.com.

Defending Criminals Can Be Hard

"The work [of a murder case] is hard to shake off. I still can't look at autopsy pictures without getting sick. There's only so much of the evil you can view without becoming burned out. You absorb it, and that's not good. My father once said: 'To keep our society free and democratic, someone has to do your job, and do it well.' Then he paused and said: 'I'm just really sorry it's you.' I feel the same way."

John Henry Browne, quoted in Rory Carroll and Simon Hattenstone, "Defending the Indefensible? Lawyers on Representing Clients Accused of Nightmarish Crimes," *Guardian*, June 27, 2014. www.theguardian.com.

people who are charged with crimes. The first group, prosecutors, represents the government. Based on evidence gathered by law enforcement, prosecutors decide whether to file charges and what charges to file. They also argue the case in court, if the case reaches that stage, and they seek a specific punishment for those who are found guilty of a crime. The second group, defense lawyers, tries to ensure that their clients get a fair trial. They are an advocate for the accused; their job is to use all legal means available to clear the defendant of charges.

Civil cases usually involve private disputes between individuals or organizations. These disputes involve a plaintiff and a defendant. The plaintiff is someone who files a lawsuit against a person, business, or government agency; and the defendant is the entity named in the lawsuit. Civil cases can involve property or money disputes, divorce or child custody issues, and liability for damages resulting from a car accident, among other things. People involved in both sides of a lawsuit hire lawyers to represent them.

What You Will Do

In 2015 the majority of lawyers worked in private practice—either for themselves or in firms employing multiple lawyers. Some of these lawyers are trial lawyers. Trial lawyers argue cases in court before a judge or jury. Typically, trial lawyers must draft opening and closing statements. They also have to decide what questions to ask and which witnesses to call to support their case. The job can be both exhilarating and frustrating. A 2016 blog on the website law360.com discussed problems lawyers encounter in trials. NY attorney Ethan Horwitz admitted, "What you plan for is easy. It's what you don't see coming that's a nightmare." Horwitz said his trial nightmare came when a client suddenly admitted he had lied about the facts, pretty much destroying the case.

Not all lawyers are trial lawyers. Many never, or almost never, go to court. In fact, their job is to make sure their clients don't ever end up in court. These lawyers usually specialize in a specific area of law—for example, tax, real estate, or corporate law. Their job is to advise their clients on various legal matters. They might draft legal documents and review legal agreements. Many large companies hire in-house lawyers so they will always be available to advise them on legal situations and to make sure their business practices do not violate any laws. Government attorneys also work by advising elected officials on legal matters, including whether laws officials propose are legal.

Whether lawyers specialize in criminal or civil law, they spend a lot of time researching the laws that pertain to their cases. They may spend hours searching through law books for other, similar cases and rulings. All of this information can be used to formulate arguments and tactics and help them draft complaints, briefs, and motions.

Law School

Patience is a virtue for anyone who wants to become a lawyer. That's because lawyers go through a lot of schooling. Many graduate from college with a bachelor's degree in English, business, political science, or economics. Then they apply to law school. Law school generally lasts three years and results in a law degree. But even after you graduate from law school, you still have to pass an examination to practice law in the state in which you want to be employed. Those exams are difficult. If you do not pass the first time, you can take the test again. Those who don't pass the exam can't work as a lawyer even if they've earned a law degree.

What Qualities Make a Lawyer?

It takes a lot of different qualities to be a lawyer. Lawyers need excellent verbal and written skills and must be able to think quickly and creatively. Lawyers must also have good people skills. Being a good judge of character helps too. Law work also involves the ability to see the big picture while at the same time drilling down on lots of facts and details. In a 2014 Quora.com blog, Houston attorney Doyle wrote that because legal work can be challenging—and sometimes tedious—"good lawyers have to possess high reserves of energy and determination—it's not a good profession for quitters."

The Best and Worst Parts of the Job

If you like helping people, being a lawyer will satisfy that desire. Elizabeth Joy Fossel, an attorney in Grand Rapids, Michigan, remarked in a 2013 *ABA Journal* article, "The true reason I went to law school was to help people who are really in a pickle." You can even help people who cannot afford to hire lawyers. Like many lawyers, Fossel does pro bono work, a legal term that means she donates her legal expertise to people who cannot afford to hire a lawyer. She usually does 100 to 250 pro bono hours a year helping people in all types of cases.

Other positive aspects of being a lawyer include the exhilaration you get from winning a legal battle. Sometimes that comes from winning money for a client or successfully defending against a criminal charge. The high pay and social standing lawyers generally have will also make you feel good about choosing this career.

Most legal cases revolve around conflicting views of how laws are interpreted and applied, what took place or didn't in a given

She Loves Her Work

"There are several things I love about my career choice. I am proud to help families that truly need it. To assist a grandmother that has reared her grandchild for several years finally get legal guardianship is rewarding. Walking out of a special education meeting with a family knowing that my presence was able to secure much needed valuable services for their child is indescribable."

Christina Kirk, quoted in Brittney Helmrich, "7 Lawyers on What They Love (and Hate) About Their Jobs," *Business News Daily*, September 28, 2015. www.businessnewsdaily.com.

situation, and what the outcome should be. That means you'll spend a lot of time battling another lawyer to win a case for your client—so you really have to like the adversarial life. In a 2015 *Business News Daily* article, Chicago attorney Lyndsay A. Markley admitted, "My job is inherently adversarial and there are entire days—and when on trial, weeks—spent fighting with opposing counsel, a judge, or other third parties." Losing is also something lawyers have to get used to because nobody wins every case.

There are other downsides to working as lawyer. One is the threat of legal action for how you handled a case. Clients sometimes sue a lawyer for malpractice if they believe he or she did a poor job in representing them. Likewise, for those who work in private practice, collecting fees from clients can sometimes be a problem.

Earnings

Many lawyers earn a good living. The US Bureau of Labor Statistics (BLS) reported that in 2015 the annual mean wage for lawyers was $136,260. Mean wage is the midpoint of income, meaning that half of the nation's lawyers made more and half made less than that amount. Lawyers who work in large cities generally make more money than those in smaller communities because there are more opportunities and more cases involving large sums of money. Lawyers employed by the government usually make less than those in private practices. However, if you become a government lawyer, you will have more job security and better benefits like health insurance and retirement. Your income will also depend on what kind of law you practice. Trial lawyers are paid the most, and some of them make millions of dollars each year. That is because they are key to winning cases that can involve huge sums of money or whether their client goes to jail.

Future Job Opportunities for Lawyers

The American Bar Association reported that in 2015 there were 1.3 million licensed lawyers in the United States. The bureau also said the number of lawyers is expected to grow 6 percent through 2024, which is the average for all occupations. However, it noted that strong competition for jobs will continue because more students graduate from law school each year than there are jobs available.

Find Out More

Above the Law
website: http://abovethelaw.com

This site has articles and information about all aspects of being a lawyer, including required education.

American Bar Association
321 N. Clark St.
Chicago, IL 60654
phone: (312) 988-5000
website: www.americanbar.org

This association for lawyers and law students has more than four hundred thousand members.

Lawyer Education

website: www.lawyeredu.org

This website has information on becoming a lawyer, including the educational and professional requirements needed in each state.

Marquette Lawyer

website: https://law.marquette.edu

This Marquette University Law School magazine has interesting articles on lawyers, law education, and the legal profession.

Pro Bono Net

website: www.probono.net

This website is about lawyers who work for free to help clients who cannot pay for legal help.

Social Activist

On October 8, 2015, students from several Philadelphia high schools walked out of class to protest budget cuts they believed were hurting their education. Cy Wolfe, a senior at the Philadelphia High School for the Creative and Performing Arts, explained at the time, "We just want to let people know students around the district will feel the effects. If we don't raise our voice, then who will?" Wolfe and his fellow student protesters could be considered social activists in the making. The desire to change something you believe is wrong, and the willingness to act on that desire, is a form of social activism. And, believe it or not, some people actually make a career out of social activism.

Most social activists work for nonprofit organizations. These groups are devoted to many different political, economic, environmental, religious, or social causes. Some, like Feeding America, focus on reducing hunger. Others, like Habitat for Humanity, build affordable housing for poor and homeless people. Some activists work mostly or exclusively in the United States. Others work in countries all over the world.

Although many social activists are volunteers, there are also many career opportunities. Career choices for social activists include being a social worker, a fund-raiser for a charity, or a lobbyist trying to create political change on various issues. Other jobs include working with social media to publicize activist work, helping seniors or people who do not speak English deal with government agencies to get needed services, and coordinating activities to clean up the environment. Social activists stock and run food pantries to feed the hungry and operate free clinics to provide health care.

Changing the World

You may be drawn to social activism because it fulfills your personal need to help people or fight for something you believe in. Nick Macdonald has done humanitarian relief work in Europe and Central Asia and now works in Portland, Oregon, advising activist groups on how to do their work better. Macdonald, in his book *Getting Your First Job in Relief and Development,* discusses his experiences of helping people around the world. He also explains

Twitter as a Tool for Social Activism

"Twitter specifically has been interesting because we're able to get feedback and responses in real time. If we think about this as community building, and we think of community building as a manifestation of love, and we think about love being about accountability, and accountability about justice, what's interesting is that Twitter has kept us honest. There's a democracy of feedback. I've had really robust conversations with people who aren't physically in the space, but who have such great ideas. And that's proven to be invaluable."

DeRay Mckesson, quoted in Noah Berlatsky, "Hashtag Activism Isn't a Cop-Out," *Atlantic,* January 7, 2015. www.theatlantic.com.

A Habitat for Humanity volunteer helps build a house for a low-income family. Nonprofit organizations such as this rely on volunteers but also have paid staff who do a variety of jobs that help fulfill the group's mission.

why such work is so rewarding: "I count myself very lucky to be able to make a living doing work that is in alignment with my values and the things that I believe in. [There] is an upside to [doing] work that you feel passionately about, and are not doing simply because you are getting paid to."

There are many places you can find social activist jobs. However, the majority of private-sector jobs are with charities and nonprofit organizations. Organizations such as the Salvation Army, Feeding America, and Habitat For Humanity raise money and provide services people need like food, clothing, and housing. Nonprofits, which include religious organizations, try to make life better for people in a variety of ways. Doctors Without Borders is an international group that provides medical care for people who live in parts of the world that lack adequate health care. Human Rights Watch works internationally to publicize and end situations in which people are denied basic human rights caused by racism, religious intolerance, or repressive governments.

Community organizer is one of the most important activist jobs. Organizations involved in every phase of social activism need someone to unite people and lead them in dealing with social issues like racism, gun violence, and inadequate housing. Terry Mizrahi is a professor at Hunter College's Silberman School of Social Work. She writes that organizers "are a necessary and vital part of a democratic form of government." Community organizers perform a variety of tasks, including meeting with the news media and speaking to groups of citizens to raise public awareness of problems they are trying to correct, such as discrimination or poverty. Organizers contact government officials to persuade them to help their cause. They also plan protests and other public events to build support to accomplish their objectives, such as feeding the hungry, ending sexual discrimination, or improving the environment.

One broad category of activist jobs is providing community and social services to people who need them, such as public housing, education, and physical and mental health care. The US Bureau of Labor Statistics (BLS) reported that in 2014 more than 1.9 million people were engaged in such work. You could work at a homeless shelter, operate a food bank, or staff a free medical clinic. If you want to concentrate on changing laws or government policy, you could work for political or special interest groups like the Sierra Club, which seeks to improve the environment.

Actually, you can be a social activist in almost any career you wish to pursue. Charities and nonprofits need accountants, lawyers, and workers with many other job skills. Even people working in the arts can be activists. Haskell Wexler won two Oscars for cinematography. When Wexler died on December 27, 2015, he was hailed as a social activist because movies he filmed reflected his activist principles like opposing war. One obituary included this statement by Wexler on why he incorporated such themes in his movies: "We have a responsibility to show the public the kinds of truths that they don't see on the TV news or the Hollywood film."

Getting into Social Activism

Amherst College has some good advice if you want to be a social activist. The website for its social activism degree program states that "the key to creating a career in activism is to find ways to bring your beliefs and values into your work." So look for jobs that involve issues that interest you, whether it is protecting endangered species, feeding hungry people, or aiding victims of violence or sexual abuse. If you do that, you will be motivated to work hard every day.

Start working as a social activist today by volunteering for a cause that appeals to you, whether it is collecting food for the poor, participating in student government or political campaigns, or raising money for charities. You could also take part in protests on issues that are meaningful to you. Those experiences will help you discover if social activist is a career you would like. You should also take classes or participate in activities that sharpen your writing and speaking skills because both are important for social activists. Expertise in using social media like Twitter is another way social activists can communicate their message to the public.

Some colleges offer degrees in social activism that include subjects like political science, sociology, government, the history of social protest, and how to recruit and organize people for activist causes. Amherst College's website on its political activism program notes that "the range of opportunities to do this [type of work] is vast and diverse" and that the classes it offers "create opportunities for [students] to develop the professional skills and knowledge they need to make a positive impact on issues they care about."

Barack Obama, Community Organizer

"It's as a consequence of working with this organization and this community that I found my calling. There was something more than making money and getting a fancy degree. The measure of my life would be public service."

Barack Obama, quoted in David Moberg, "Barack Obama's Political Vision Grew Out of His Early Experiences as a Community Organizer in Chicago," *Nation*, April 3, 2007. www.thenation.com.

The Best and Worst Parts of Social Activism

The greatest satisfaction you will get from a social activist job is that your work will improve life for society as a whole or for certain groups of people. Your job will let you meet people from all walks of life. You can work locally if you want or look for a job that will allow you to travel and experience life in foreign countries. Project Hope and other organizations work in many countries to provide people with humanitarian relief. You will often have to fight hard to achieve something, whether it is creating a new program to help people or changing a bad government policy. The thrill of accomplishing your goal will make you ecstatic.

Pay for social activism work is low, and conditions can be difficult. You might work in places with substandard living conditions, and your life might even be endangered by crime, war, or religious violence. Being surrounded daily by poverty, violence, sickness, and death can make you sad even while you are trying to alleviate those conditions. Felicia Davis is an environmental activist who created the Historically Black Colleges and Universities Green Fund, which is improving energy use at black schools. Davis loves activist work. But in a 2015 Internet story, she warned that doing such work can be emotionally draining: "Activists [who] must encounter death, devastation and enormous human suffering are very special people that have a unique capacity to work through these tragedies."

Starting Early

"One of my earliest recollections in the public sphere was as a four-year-old marching with my mother in Englewood, NJ, protesting public school segregation. At 13 my very first campaign was an effort to raise funds to support drug treatment then unavailable at our local hospital. [My] father taught me African history, my mother taught me that we have healing power, and my grandmother taught me that we each have a duty to serve."

Felicia Davis, quoted in Ann Brown, "Activism as a Career? Yes, You Can!," Madame Noire, August 12, 2015. http://madamenoire.com.

How Much Money Can I Earn as a Social Activist?

One sacrifice you may have to make as a social activist is to earn less money than you might at other jobs you are qualified for. Many people accept lower salaries because they feel it is more important to help people. However, there are many different social activism organizations and jobs, and some positions pay well. The BLS lists many activist jobs under the broad heading of community and social service occupations. These jobs include mental health, rehabilitation, substance abuse, and school counselors. Other social activist jobs include health care workers, social workers, and substance abuse counselors. The BLS reported that the mean annual wage for 1.9 million such jobs in 2014 was $45,310, which means that half the workers made more and half made less than that amount. But there are even more activist jobs with charities and nonprofit organizations. Although some social activist pay is low, some jobs with large charities or nonprofit organizations can be financially rewarding if you have advanced skills in computers or other technical areas.

Future Opportunities

Social activist job opportunities are expected to grow in the future. In 2014 the BLS predicted that the wide-ranging job category of community and social service occupations will grow 10 percent through 2024, which is faster than the average for all occupations. The growth is due to increases in the number of senior citizens who need care and the demand for health-related services. Other factors, including a growing political divide in the nation, should also lead to increased job opportunities in activist work.

Find Out More

Amherst College
website: www.amherst.edu

This college website has information on social activism and the social activist courses it offers.

Idealist Careers
website: http://idealistcareers.org

This website has blogs, information, and links to other sites about careers in social activism.

Nonprofit Quarterly
website: https://nonprofitquarterly.org

This independent, nonprofit news organization offers information about nonprofit social activist work.

Partnership for Public Service
website: http://ourpublicservice.org

This is a nonprofit, nonpartisan group that works with federal agencies and private groups to help college students who want to perform public service get jobs that suit them.

Popular Resistance
website: www.popularresistance.org

Since 2011 this website has featured stories, blogs, and other information about social activist activities around the nation.

Teacher/Professor

Almost everyone has a favorite teacher—someone they remember fondly for teaching them how to write with style, look at a mathematical theory in a new way, or think critically about political posturing during a presidential election year. Talk about job satisfaction. What other profession allows an individual to impart knowledge that will be cherished long after the lesson is complete? Reverend Jeffrey T. LaBelle knows this feeling. The Jesuit priest has been teaching since 1979. During that time he has taught high school English, Spanish, and world history. He's also taught education courses at the university level. In an interview with the author, LaBelle said his greatest joy when teaching occurs when "I see the light come on in my students' eyes when they have an insight, make a connection to what I am teaching them."

The Work of Teachers and Professors

Teaching is about imparting knowledge as well as helping young people learn to make connections, think for themselves, and take their place as fully participating members of society. This is where your fascination with government and politics kicks in. In your studies, you've developed the ability to think critically, to evaluate other points of view, to solve problems, and to clearly communicate ideas. As a teacher you can pass along these same skills to your students. At the elementary school level, educators teach young boys and girls the basic skills they need in life, such as reading, mathematics, and a basic knowledge of history, literature, and science. Secondary school teachers provide students with more advanced knowledge and skills in English, history, math, and science as well as other subjects including foreign languages. Many classes are intended to help students gain the knowledge they need to prepare for life after high school, including qualifying for more advanced education. Teachers at colleges and universities instruct their students in a wide variety of subjects that prepare them for all sorts of professions.

Much of your time will be spent teaching students in a classroom setting. Most elementary school teachers instruct students in multiple subjects unless they have been trained to teach a specialized subject like art. In secondary schools, teachers often specialize in a single subject like mathematics, biology, foreign languages, or history. Teaching can take many forms: lecturing on various subjects, showing students how to solve math problems,

A Long Day

"I stay after school four days a week to help students make up work, get extra help on writing assignments, or just work on problems they are having with the material. Most of the teachers at my school stay after to offer extra help. It's not really a formal arrangement, but it seems to work. Right before I leave, I make sure the room is clean and my desk clear."

Julia G. Thompson, "A Day in the Life of a High School English Teacher," Teaching. http://teaching.monster.com.

Why Be a Teacher?

"I teach because I enjoy helping people be successful. I enjoy seeing a light bulb come on in a kid's eye—whether it's in the classroom, or in life in general. I talk to the kids not just about math, but about life. If we can reach them in any one of those avenues, I feel I can help someone achieve their goals and dreams. I feel some of them may even start dreaming, because they never thought they had the possibility for it before."

David Crumm, quoted in Joselyn King, "Teachers Explain: 'Why I Teach,'" *Intelligencer*, November 29, 2015. www.theintelligencer.net/page/content.detail/id/648036/Teachers -Explain---Why-I-Teach-.html.

or demonstrating how to repair an automobile engine. Teachers instruct large groups of students, but they also sometimes work with individual students who are having trouble learning.

Teaching in the classroom is just one part of being a teacher. Most teachers spend several hours each week outside of classroom hours preparing lectures and daily lesson plans. These plans guide them as they teach something specific each day, such as how to use fractions in mathematics. Teachers also make long-range lesson plans on what they are teaching students. A teacher's day may include meetings with a principal, other teachers, or parents. Teachers also have to do a lot of paperwork, from grading papers and tests to filling out report cards; such work is often done at home after school or on the weekend. Teachers also have to document that they have taught their students mandated elements of the curriculum. Teachers also may have to supervise students during nonclassroom periods, which may include going outside during recess or helping students get on the right bus to go home when school ends. Teachers sometimes have to stay after school to help students or meet with other teachers or parents. They sometimes have to assist with student athletic activities, music programs, and trips to museums and other educational places that take place outside of regular school hours.

How Do I Become a Teacher or Professor?

You will generally need a bachelor's degree to become a teacher. Most teachers major in education because they want to prepare for this career. However, most states have programs that allow teachers to teach without an education major if they have the knowledge required to teach a certain subject. For example, if a prospective teacher majored in mathematics or history, he or she would be qualified to teach those subjects. In addition, public school teachers in all fifty states, the District of Columbia, and Puerto Rico must have a state-issued certificate or license to show they are qualified to teach. Qualifications for such certificates vary and may include having a degree in a particular subject to teach it. Teachers are generally licensed to teach students at various stages of their education: early childhood education (preschool through third grade), elementary education (first through sixth grade), middle school (usually fifth through eighth grade), and secondary (usually a specific subject from seventh through twelfth grade). Postsecondary teachers have advanced degrees in the subjects they teach, with a master's degree being the minimum.

The Best and Worst Parts of Teaching

Lisa Meincke is a third-grade teacher at Lakeview Elementary in Whitewater, Wisconsin. During an interview with the author, Meincke said that the best times when teaching are "those 'light bulb' moments. You work SO hard and when there is success you feel like you finally did it (the kids too!)." If you become a teacher, you will get to experience that same personal satisfaction of seeing students learn something, especially those who struggle in school. Another joy of teaching is hearing former students praise you years later for what you taught them. In an interview with the author, LaBelle said, "I have the joy of hearing from my students now and then, [and I] enjoy learning of their successes in various professions and endeavors."

A major benefit of teaching is that you have more time off than most workers. Elementary and secondary schools generally operate on a 180-day year, a total that is fewer days than most full-time jobs require from workers. In a district with a traditional school year, teachers often have a short break at Christmas and Easter and then a long summer vacation. Even if they work at a school on a year-round schedule, teachers still have a lot of time off. In the most common year-round schedule, teachers work in 45-day blocks and then have 15 days off.

You may find that low pay is one of the worst parts of being a teacher. Like other government employees, teachers generally earn less than someone with the same education in the private sector. As a result, they may work a second job for part of their summer vacation or during other breaks. Natalie Klem is a fifth-grade teacher at Lead Prep Southeast in Nashville, Tennessee. In a 2015 *Atlantic* magazine story about low pay, Klem said, "I can't remember the last summer I didn't work."

Low salaries are one reason why many teachers feel they are not respected for the work they do. Richard Ingersoll is a professor of education at the University of Pennsylvania. In a 2013 *Atlantic* magazine article, Ingersoll said he quit teaching high school social studies and algebra after six years because "it's just a lack

Teaching Students of Different Ages

"I like teaching young people at all levels from ninth grade through graduate school. Each age group and level has its blessings. The younger students bring joy to me because they learn and grow more dramatically in their knowledge. The graduate students bring more intellectual satisfaction because of their unique and thought-provoking insights and perspectives. They help stimulate my ongoing curiosity to learn more and view things from new perspectives."

Jeffrey T. LaBelle, quoted in an interview with the author, December 10, 2015.

of respect. Teachers in schools do not call the shots. [They're] told what to do; it's a very disempowered line of work." Ingersoll was referring to laws and other directives from various levels of government that mandate what teachers must teach. However, teachers also have to take orders from school principals, even if they disagree with them.

Something else you may not like is filling out a lot of forms to prove that you have met government-imposed teaching standards on various subjects or issues. That paperwork is often done after class or at home on days off. Even though you will work fewer days than most full-time workers, you will have to work at various tasks outside the regular school day. Your extra hours will include grading papers and report cards, talking and meeting with parents, and returning to school at night for concerts and other school events.

How Much Can I Earn as a Teacher or Professor?

After earning a college degree, you may be disappointed at your starting salary as a teacher. The website PayScale reported in November 2015 that nationally teachers in elementary through secondary school average $37,005 the first year they teach, a total lower than that of college graduates in many other careers. Nonetheless, their salaries will steadily rise through the years as they gain more experience. Teachers in many school districts can also boost their pay by getting advanced degrees. If they teach at the college level, their pay will be higher than for lower levels of education. A professor's salary will rise by experience and whether he or she becomes a full professor. The median salary for a profession is the amount of salary in which half the workers in that career make either more or less than that amount. The US Bureau of Labor Statistics (BLS) The US Bureau of Labor Statistics (BLS) reported that in 2015 the median annual salary for elementary teachers was $54,550; for secondary teachers it was $57,200; and for postsecondary teachers, $74,720. Salaries were also generally higher at public rather than private/parochial elementary and secondary schools.

Future Outlook

If you are considering becoming a teacher, the BLS has some good news for you. Currently there are nearly 1 million teaching jobs in the United States. The BLS reports that in 2014 there were 948,960 elementary and secondary teachers in public and private schools and 1.3 million postsecondary teachers. And the bureau predicts that the number of new teachers needed will grow through 2022 by 12 percent for elementary, 6 percent for high school, and 19 percent for postsecondary teachers. Those figures are all above average for job growth in other careers. The reason schools need people like you is simple—there is a growing shortage of teachers. Ana Margarita Sanchez graduated in 2015 with a master's degree in education from Stanford University. In a *New York Times* story, Sanchez admitted that she "was definitely taken aback at the intensity" of how eager school systems were to hire her. Sanchez settled on a job teaching fourth grade in a bilingual school in San Francisco. In the future, you may be the new teacher school systems are looking for.

Find Out More

Association of American Educators
website: www.aaeteachers.org

This nonunion website includes information on how to become a teacher, what the job is like, and practices that promote good teaching.

Education World
website: www.educationworld.com

This online resource for educators features education news and a variety of resources to help teachers improve their skills.

Edutopia
website: www.edutopia.org

This George Lucas Foundation website has blogs and videos about teachers, how to teach, and positive things happening in education.

How Can I Become a Teacher?

website: http://teach.com

This website explains the education a teacher needs, experiences teachers have had, and other information on this career.

National Education Association

website: www.nea.org

The National Education Association, which has 3 million members from preschool to university-level educators, promotes teaching as a profession.

Urban Planner

A Few Facts

Number of Jobs

There were 35,280 jobs in 2014 for urban and regional planners

Pay

Median pay for urban planners in 2014 was $69,010

Education

A minimum of a master's degree

Where the Jobs Are

About two-thirds of urban planners work for government agencies at the local, state, and federal levels

Future Outlook

Job growth through 2022 is estimated at 10 percent

If streets are laid out haphazardly, it is hard to drive from one area to another. When large population shifts occur within a community, new schools and other services for citizens are needed there. Communities also deal with factors like economics, the environment, and the recreational needs of its citizens that can change over time and create a variety of problems for local governments and the citizens they serve. Urban planners help governments on all levels deal with such problems by taking action to alleviate or fix them. They also constantly keep track of such factors so they can anticipate future problems and act before they begin to lessen the quality of life in their communities. Thus, urban planners are vital in making communities better places to live, whether that means building new roads, updating water and sewer systems, or strengthening the local economy by wise use of available land.

So if you think it would be rewarding to help communities remain good places to live or even improve the lifestyles of local residents, being an urban planner could be a career you should consider.

The title of urban planner makes the job sound simple—you make plans for the future growth of an area so that it will remain a good and pleasant place to live. However, creating a plan for the future growth of any area—whether it is a city, suburb, rural area, or an entire region—is very complex. In a 2014 blog on govtech.com, award-winning Canadian urban planner John G. Jung explained how hard the task really is: "As planning concerns itself with everything around it [the planner] must take a true 360 degree, all-encompassing look at everything related to its development."

Urban planners do this by being able to envision alternative ways to structure the physical and social environment to make it a better place for people to live. That "all-encompassing look" that an urban planner makes includes human needs such as where future residents will live as well as economic concerns about the location of new businesses from factories to shops and offices. The economic part of their plan also has to estimate how many new jobs will be created to ensure that new residents will be employed. They also have to consider future transportation needs involving automobiles, trains, planes, and even ships. Other aspects of their plan include environmental factors like how to maintain sufficient supplies of energy while still keeping air and water clean. The American Planning Association (APA) states that any

What Is Urban Planning?

"Urban planning is not a science; it's a combination of the arts, science, philosophy, sociology, economics and politics. Its theories and practices, delivered in the form of plans, are a reflection of a language focused on the use of land by its citizens and the design of the urban environment upon which the site is to be developed on as well as reflected in its impact on the surrounding area."

John G. Jung, "Urban Planners and the Revolutionary City," *Digital Communities* (blog), Govtech.com, July 21, 2014. www.govtech.com.

plans an urban planner makes must also include "places where people want to be," such as parks and golf courses. The APA explains that they are important because "people choose where to live, work, and play based on many factors, and the physical design of urban places is one of those factors [and they] can either attract or repel people and investment in the community."

About two-thirds of planner jobs are with different levels of government. Most jobs are at the city or county level, but you could also work for a regional, state, or federal agency. There are also jobs in the private sector with consulting firms, which are often hired by the government, as well as with developers of housing and business projects.

What Would I Do as an Urban Planner?

The desired result of politics and government is to make life better for citizens. Urban planners play an important role in doing this by creating more efficient, economical, and positive ways to handle a variety of social, economic, business, and environmental problems. Their goal is to make life better for people living in the area they are responsible for planning. Many planners work in urban areas, but others work in rural, suburban, or larger regional areas. However, the job of urban planner in any area, no matter how big or small, is the same: to plan the area's future growth or how to better utilize its current resources.

The plan an urban planner creates could involve new highways or roads to move traffic more efficiently or greener ways to dispose of garbage and waste to protect the environment. Likewise, the planner might have to draw up a plan to boost economic development. Such plans will create more jobs for residents, and new businesses will also increase tax dollars to fund government. The plan might even focus on the need for more parks, golf courses, and other recreation areas that help people enjoy life.

Urban planners create plans on how to best use available land for residential, business, and other purposes; meet future transportation needs; and determine what economic development will

The goal of urban planners is to create livable communities. To do this, they have to consider all different aspects of daily living, including transportation, water, shopping areas, housing, playgrounds, and more.

benefit the community the most. But devising plans to improve living conditions in an area is only one part of an urban planner's job. To make the plan a reality, the planner has to win approval of it from both government officials, who have the power to enact it, and local residents, who fund it with their tax dollars and could kill it by opposing the plan.

When meeting with officials and citizens, urban planners have to convince them to support their plan; that can be in private meetings with one or two people or public hearings where hundreds show up to voice their opinions. Joel Dietl heads the planning department in the city of Franklin, Wisconsin. In an interview with the author, Dietl said planners have to know how to win support from officials and key public leaders. Those skills are different from having the knowledge to draw up such plans, but according to Dietl, "The higher up the ladder you go [as a planner] the more important your people skills become." That is because when you are the head of planning, you are responsible for winning approval of the plans.

Preparation for Urban Planning Jobs

SimCity is an open-ended computer game focused on building a city. If you think you might want to become an urban planner, you should play it. The APA claims that "since 1989, scores of children and adults have been introduced to the field of urban planning through the computer game SimCity." That's because players have to perform tasks that urban planners do in real life, such as deciding how much land to set aside for housing, industry, and commercial buildings. The game shows you how your decisions affect growth of the city, from the amount of taxes the city generates to how much pollution it creates. Cities need tax dollars to fund government but on the other hand also want to limit pollution to improve the environment and curb health problems for its citizens. So this game is a way to see if you enjoy doing such tasks.

If you decide you want to be an urban planner, you will need to attend a college or university that offers a major in planning. A bachelor's degree in planning is generally required for planning jobs. However, the Association of Collegiate Schools of Planning recommends getting at least a master's degree if you want to get the best jobs in this field.

The APA says you should consider this profession if you are good at making plans and evaluating future projects. You should also be good at solving problems by using a blend of technical expertise, creativity, and common sense. You must be able to resolve conflicts with coworkers as well as other people, from government officials to members of the general public, whose approval you have to win for plans you create.

The Best and Worst Parts of the Job

One reason why you may want to become an urban planner is that you can positively affect how people in your community live.